Police Officers

Julie Murray

Abdo

MY COMMUNITY: JOBS

Kids

abdopublishing.com

Published by Abdo Kids, a division of ABDO, PO Box 398166, Minneapolis, Minnesota 55439.
Copyright © 2016 by Abdo Consulting Group, Inc. International copyrights reserved in all countries.
No part of this book may be reproduced in any form without written permission from the publisher.

Printed in the United States of America, North Mankato, Minnesota.

052015

092015

Photo Credits: iStock, Shutterstock, © cdrin p.13, Leonard Zhukovsky p.22 / Shutterstock.com

Production Contributors: Teddy Borth, Jennie Forsberg, Grace Hansen

Design Contributors: Candice Keimig, Dorothy Toth

Library of Congress Control Number: 2014958407

Cataloging-in-Publication Data

Murray, Julie.
 Police officers / Julie Murray.
  p. cm. -- (My community: jobs)
ISBN 978-1-62970-916-1
Includes index.
1. Police--Juvenile literature. 2. Police patrol--Juvenile literature. I. Title.
363.2--dc23
                  2014958407

Table of Contents

Police Officers

Police officers keep us safe.

They make sure laws are followed.

They help people.

Sam must cross the street safely.

They make sure people drive safely. Jane was driving too fast. She gets a ticket.

Some police ride in cars.

Others ride bikes or horses.

Here comes the police car! The
siren is loud. The lights flash.

5 PCT 1482

NYPD
Courtesy
Professionalism
Respect

15

Police wear uniforms.

They have tool belts.

Some police work with dogs.

The dogs help them!

Do you know a police officer?

A Police Officer's Tools

flashlight

patrol car

handcuffs

two-way radio

Glossary

laws

the set of rules made by the government of a town, state, country, etc.

ticket

a piece of paper that tells you that you have wrongly driven or parked your car.

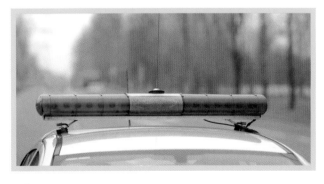

siren

a piece of equipment that makes a very loud warning sound.

Index

abdokids.com

Use this code to log on to abdokids.com and access crafts, games, videos, and more!

Abdo Kids Code:
MPK9161